D1518473

The U.S. Armed Forces

U.S. Marine Expeditionary Units

by Carrie A. Braulick

Consultant:
Barbara J. Fox
Reading Specialist
North Carolina State University

Capstone *press*

Mankato, Minnesota

Blazers is published by Capstone Press,
151 Good Counsel Drive, P.O. Box 669, Mankato, Minnesota 56002.
www.capstonepress.com

Library of Congress Cataloging-in-Publication Data
Braulick, Carrie A., 1975–
U.S. Marine expeditionary units / by Carrie A. Braulick.
p. cm.—(Blazers. The U.S. Armed Forces)
Summary: "Describes the U.S. Marine Expeditionary Units, including their
missions, vehicles, weapons, equipment, and jobs"—Provided by publisher.
Includes bibliographical references and index.
ISBN 0-7368-4395-7 (hardcover)
1. United States. Marine Corps—Organization—Juvenile literature. I. Title.
II. Series.
VE23.B73 2006
359.9'6'0973—dc22
2004028165

Credits

Juliette Peters, set designer; Patrick D. Dentinger, book designer; Jo Miller,
photo researcher; Scott Thoms, photo editor

Photo Credits

AP/Dimitri Messinis, cover (inset); The London Times/POOL, Simon Walker,
21
Corbis/Reuters, cover; Desmond Boylan, 6
George Hall/Check Six, 16–17, 20
Getty Images Inc./U.S. Navy/Richard J. Brunson, 26
Hans Halberstadt/Check Six, 22
Photo by Ted Carlson/Fotodynamics, 15 (top), 25
U.S. Marine Corps photo by Lance Cpl. Brian L. Wickliffe, 7, 8 (both)
U.S. Navy Photo by JO1 Joe Krypel, 5; JO2 Robert Sealover, 13 (bottom);
PH1 Bart Bauer, 11; PH1 Michael Lewis, 15 (bottom); PH1 Ted Banks, 12;
PH2 Christopher M. Staten, 27; PH2 Michael Sandberg, 19; PH3 Angel
Roman-Otero, 28–29; PH3 Stephanie M. Bergman, 14
Zuma/Andrew Silk, 13 (top)

**Capstone Press thanks Captain Carrie C. Batson of the 11th MEU for her
assistance in preparing this book.**

1 2 3 4 5 6 10 09 08 07 06 05

Table of Contents

MEUs in Action

Members of a Marine Expeditionary Unit (MEU) reach shore. They move equipment off a landing craft.

The Marines move away from shore. They see an enemy camp. The Marines closely watch the enemy soldiers.

The Marines attack the camp. They capture the enemy soldiers. Their mission is a success.

BLAZER FACT

Some MEU missions are secret. In 2003, MEUs did secret missions while fighting in Iraq.

MEU Vehicles

MEUs are groups of highly trained Marines. They travel on Navy ships until they go on missions.

MEUs use many vehicles on missions. Tanks carry Marines over land. Other vehicles carry Marines both over land and through water.

M1A1 tank

Light Armored Vehicle (LAV)

Assault Amphibian Vehicle (AAV)

15

AV-8B Harrier jet

BLAZER FACT

The AV-8B Harrier jet doesn't need a runway to take off. It can rise straight into the air.

Attack jets and helicopters fire missiles at enemy targets. Other aircraft carry Marines and supplies.

AH-1W Super Cobra helicopter

CH-46 Sea Knight helicopter

15

AV-8B Harrier Jet

Missile

Bombs

Air inlet

Cockpit

Nose

★ ★ ★ ★ ★ ★ ★ ★ ★ ★ ★ ★ ★

Tail

Wing

Bombs

Missile

Weapons and Equipment

Marines in MEUs carry guns. They use the powerful M16 rifle. A grenade launcher can attach to the rifle.

M16 rifle

Grenade launcher

Marines fire Stinger missiles to destroy enemy aircraft. Javelin missiles blast through heavy armor on enemy tanks.

Stinger missile system

BLAZER FACT

MEUs carry enough supplies to live on land for 15 days.

Laser designator

The equipment MEUs use depends on the mission. Laser beams from laser designators guide weapons to their targets.

MEU Jobs

Most MEU members fight on the ground. Others fly aircraft or drive vehicles.

COL. M.R. SAVARESE
"RAGU"

CAPT B.H. RITTERBY
"CRITTER"

Officers lead enlisted members in their duties. Members of MEUs train hard. They must be ready for missions at all times.

BLAZER FACT

Not all MEU missions involve combat. MEUs also help people after natural disasters.

MARINE CORPS RANKS

★ ★ ★ ★ ★ ★ ★ ★ ★ ★ ★ ★ ★ ★ ★ ★ ★

ENLISTED	OFFICERS
Private	Lieutenant
Corporal	Captain
Sergeant	Major
Staff Sergeant	Colonel
Gunnery Sergeant	General
Master Sergeant	
Master Gunnery Sergeant	

A landing craft rushes
MEU vehicles to shore

Glossary

armor (AR-mur)—a protective metal covering

camp (KAMP)—a place where soldiers gather while they are not traveling

enlisted member (en-LISS-tuhd MEM-bur)—a member of the military who is not an officer

laser beam (LAY-zur BEEM)—a narrow, powerful ray of light

missile (MISS-uhl)—an explosive that can fly long distances

mission (MISH-uhn)—a military task

officer (OF-uh-sur)—a military member who directs enlisted members in their duties

rifle (RYE-fuhl)—a powerful gun that is fired from the shoulder

runway (RUHN-way)—a strip of land that aircraft use for taking off and landing

tank (TANGK)—an armored combat vehicle equipped with heavy guns that moves on two tracks

target (TAR-git)—an object that is aimed or shot at

Read More

Cooper, Jason. *The U.S. Marine Corps.* Fighting Forces. Vero Beach, Fla.: Rourke, 2004.

Green, Michael, and Gladys Green. *The U.S. Marine Expeditionary Units at War.* On the Front Lines. Mankato, Minn.: Capstone Press, 2004.

Hopkins, Ellen. *U.S. Special Operations Forces.* U.S. Armed Forces. Chicago: Heinemann, 2004.

Internet Sites

FactHound offers a safe, fun way to find Internet sites related to this book. All of the sites on FactHound have been researched by our staff.

Here's how:

1. Visit *www.facthound.com*
2. Type in this special code **0736843957** for age-appropriate sites. Or enter a search word related to this book for a more general search.
3. Click on the **Fetch It** button.

FactHound will fetch the best sites for you!

★★★★★★★★★★★

Index